The confessions of the Countess of Strathmore; written by herself. Carefully copied from the original, lodged in Doctor's Commons.

Mary Eleanor Bowes

ECCO
PRINT EDITIONS

The confessions of the Countess of Strathmore; written by herself. Carefully copied from the original, lodged in Doctor's Commons.
Strathmore, Mary Eleanor Bowes, Countess of
ESTCID: T107400
Reproduction from British Library
With a half-title.
London : printed for W. Locke, 1793.
100p. ; 8°

Eighteenth Century
Collections Online
Print Editions

Gale ECCO Print Editions

Relive history with *Eighteenth Century Collections Online*, now available in print for the independent historian and collector. This series includes the most significant English-language and foreign-language works printed in Great Britain during the eighteenth century, and is organized in seven different subject areas including literature and language; medicine, science, and technology; and religion and philosophy. The collection also includes thousands of important works from the Americas.

The eighteenth century has been called "The Age of Enlightenment." It was a period of rapid advance in print culture and publishing, in world exploration, and in the rapid growth of science and technology – all of which had a profound impact on the political and cultural landscape. At the end of the century the American Revolution, French Revolution and Industrial Revolution, perhaps three of the most significant events in modern history, set in motion developments that eventually dominated world political, economic, and social life.

In a groundbreaking effort, Gale initiated a revolution of its own: digitization of epic proportions to preserve these invaluable works in the largest online archive of its kind. Contributions from major world libraries constitute over 175,000 original printed works. Scanned images of the actual pages, rather than transcriptions, recreate the works *as they first appeared.*

Now for the first time, these high-quality digital scans of original works are available via print-on-demand, making them readily accessible to libraries, students, independent scholars, and readers of all ages.

For our initial release we have created seven robust collections to form one the world's most comprehensive catalogs of 18th century works.

Initial Gale ECCO Print Editions collections include:

History and Geography
Rich in titles on English life and social history, this collection spans the world as it was known to eighteenth-century historians and explorers. Titles include a wealth of travel accounts and diaries, histories of nations from throughout the world, and maps and charts of a world that was still being discovered. Students of the War of American Independence will find fascinating accounts from the British side of conflict.

Social Science

Delve into what it was like to live during the eighteenth century by reading the first-hand accounts of everyday people, including city dwellers and farmers, businessmen and bankers, artisans and merchants, artists and their patrons, politicians and their constituents. Original texts make the American, French, and Industrial revolutions vividly contemporary.

Medicine, Science and Technology

Medical theory and practice of the 1700s developed rapidly, as is evidenced by the extensive collection, which includes descriptions of diseases, their conditions, and treatments. Books on science and technology, agriculture, military technology, natural philosophy, even cookbooks, are all contained here.

Literature and Language

Western literary study flows out of eighteenth-century works by Alexander Pope, Daniel Defoe, Henry Fielding, Frances Burney, Denis Diderot, Johann Gottfried Herder, Johann Wolfgang von Goethe, and others. Experience the birth of the modern novel, or compare the development of language using dictionaries and grammar discourses.

Religion and Philosophy

The Age of Enlightenment profoundly enriched religious and philosophical understanding and continues to influence present-day thinking. Works collected here include masterpieces by David Hume, Immanuel Kant, and Jean-Jacques Rousseau, as well as religious sermons and moral debates on the issues of the day, such as the slave trade. The Age of Reason saw conflict between Protestantism and Catholicism transformed into one between faith and logic -- a debate that continues in the twenty-first century.

Law and Reference

This collection reveals the history of English common law and Empire law in a vastly changing world of British expansion. Dominating the legal field is the *Commentaries of the Law of England* by Sir William Blackstone, which first appeared in 1765. Reference works such as almanacs and catalogues continue to educate us by revealing the day-to-day workings of society.

Fine Arts

The eighteenth-century fascination with Greek and Roman antiquity followed the systematic excavation of the ruins at Pompeii and Herculaneum in southern Italy; and after 1750 a neoclassical style dominated all artistic fields. The titles here trace developments in mostly English-language works on painting, sculpture, architecture, music, theater, and other disciplines. Instructional works on musical instruments, catalogs of art objects, comic operas, and more are also included.

The BiblioLife Network

This project was made possible in part by the BiblioLife Network (BLN), a project aimed at addressing some of the huge challenges facing book preservationists around the world. The BLN includes libraries, library networks, archives, subject matter experts, online communities and library service providers. We believe every book ever published should be available as a high-quality print reproduction; printed on-demand anywhere in the world. This insures the ongoing accessibility of the content and helps generate sustainable revenue for the libraries and organizations that work to preserve these important materials.

The following book is in the "public domain" and represents an authentic reproduction of the text as printed by the original publisher. While we have attempted to accurately maintain the integrity of the original work, there are sometimes problems with the original work or the micro-film from which the books were digitized. This can result in minor errors in reproduction. Possible imperfections include missing and blurred pages, poor pictures, markings and other reproduction issues beyond our control. Because this work is culturally important, we have made it available as part of our commitment to protecting, preserving, and promoting the world's literature.

GUIDE TO FOLD-OUTS MAPS and OVERSIZED IMAGES

The book you are reading was digitized from microfilm captured over the past thirty to forty years. Years after the creation of the original microfilm, the book was converted to digital files and made available in an online database.

In an online database, page images do not need to conform to the size restrictions found in a printed book. When converting these images back into a printed bound book, the page sizes are standardized in ways that maintain the detail of the original. For large images, such as fold-out maps, the original page image is split into two or more pages

Guidelines used to determine how to split the page image follows:

• Some images are split vertically; large images require vertical and horizontal splits.
• For horizontal splits, the content is split left to right.
• For vertical splits, the content is split from top to bottom.
• For both vertical and horizontal splits, the image is processed from top left to bottom right.

CONFESSIONS.

Price 2s. 6d.

THE

CONFESSIONS

OF THE

Countefs of Strathmore;

WRITTEN BY HERSELF.

CAREFULLY COPIED FROM

THE ORIGINAL,

LODGED IN

DOCTOR's COMMONS.

When hoary Age the luftful Paffions bend,
Compunction oft the Matron's bofom rend:
Then comes CONFESSION, eager to difclofe
The *fource* and *caufe* of all her prefent woes.

LONDON:

PRINTED FOR W. LOCKE, NO. 12, RED LION-STREET, HOLBORN.

1793.

CONFESSIONS.

I HAVE been guilty of five crimes.

The firſt, my unnatural diſlike to my eldeſt ſon, for faults which, at moſt, he could only be the innocent cauſe and not the author of: of this I have repented many months ago, and am moſt ſincerely ſorry I did not ſooner, in compliance with ſincere and moſt diſintereſted advice.

My ſecond crime was, my connection with Mr. Gray before Lord Strathmore's

B   death;

death; in punifhment of which very crime, God blinded my judgment, that I could not difcern, in any cafe, what was for my children's and my own advantage; but in every thing where there were two expedients, I chofe the worft.

By medicines, I have reafon to think, I mifcarried three times, and attempted it the fourth; but, thank God, failed perpetrating that crime.

Next, I repent having profaned Saint Paul's and Weftminfter Abbey, by giving Mr. Gray meetings there, before Lord Strathmore's death; and that afterwards, inftead of ufing the influence I had over him to make him a better chriftian, I rather made him worfe.

Another

Another crime was, plighting myfelf moft folemnly to Mr. Gray, at St. Paul's, to marry none but him; and yet I married you, which, together with my previous connection with you, I reckon amongft my crimes.

I am now going to enumerate my imprudencies; firft declaring, I have told you every crime I ever was guilty of, and that I never had a criminal connection with any perfon but yourfelf and Mr. Gray, and that Mr. James Graham was the only one, befides, who could have ftood the leaft chance of fucceeding in fuch an attempt: yet violent as my paffion was for him, I do ftill fincerely think it was pure; for my anxiety about his health and welfare continued two years after he left England, though I never faw or heard from him

during

during that time, or received a meffage from him by his fifter above twice, though fhe always wrote about him.

Of my imprudencies I fhall now give you an exact account, under general heads, as you defired; referring for your in-fpection, in cafe you chufe to fee it, a moft circumftantial account of every thought and action of my life, which I am drawing up.

I was imprudent, though moft inno-cent, both in thought and deed, in my flirtation—when quite a girl, with the Duke of Buccleugh's brother, which lafted but a very fhort time. I was imprudent in marrying Lord Strathmore, againft my mother's advice, though with her con-fent.

I was

I was so imprudent, as to give very improper encouragement to Mr. James Graham, and to give him reason, by indirect, though plain words, to think that I had more than an affectionate friendship for him; and that I had once, I confess, and was weak enough, during a fortnight that he lived under the same roof, and were much together, to admit from him many improper declarations, not only without anger, but even with satisfaction. After he went out of Scotland, I received one letter from him only, which I burnt to ashes, and drank them up for fear of any accident· I never wrote to him but once, which was in a feigned hand, and what none but himself could understand: this was in a cover of his sister's letter, which reached him all torn to pieces, and long after the time it ought; so that it

was

was quite unintelligible, and I never after that wrote to him except once, all before he left London. We often fent fuch meffages, as we could with fafety, to each other, through his fifter's means; who all the time protefted fhe would not do fuch a thing, and made Mrs. Parifh believe the affection was all on my fide—that fhe wifhed to diffuade me from fuch thoughts, and refufed to write any meffage, which I believe fhe thinks to this moment; and that Mifs Graham is a moft virtuous woman and true friend, which is fo much, I know, the very reverfe of her character, that after I was thoroughly acquainted with it, nothing fhould have induced me to keep up a correfpondence, or the leaft acquaintance with her, but my paffion for her brother, and the ufe fhe was of to me in it.

At

At length I thought he uſed me very ill, and after complaining of it without redreſs (though I have reaſon to believe Miſs G. concealed a letter, if not more, of his from me) I wrote a very violent letter to Miſs G. full of abuſe of her bro-ther; and concluding, with deſiring ſhe would retail it to him, and add, that he might ‘ aller ſe faire pendre.’ This hurt her exceedingly, and having no occaſion for ſuch a troubleſome woman, I was glad to get rid of her correſpondence.

When he came to ſee me in London after this, (which was after Lord Strath-more’s death) and waited on me, I would not ſee him, and he attempted to throw himſelf in my way to no purpoſe. I was then engaged to Mr. Gray, and having, at the riſk of my life, conquered my

head-

headstrong passion, I was determined not to expose myself to another conflict, with one whom I had so much reason to be afraid of.

I was more than imprudent in encouraging and keeping company with people of such execrable and infamous principles: though, indeed, I did not think them such then; but that is no excuse for me, as I ought not to have trusted or allowed any body to have frequented my house, without a previous long acquaintance. It was still worse, to let George so much into my secrets. As to my madness, in wishing Mrs. Stephens to stay with me after I was married, I can only say, that it was a diabolical infatuation, and that had I known her as I do now, I should not only have intreated you to turn her out

of

of the houſe directly; and have confeſſed, that ſuch a wretch was not fit to live on the earth; and had I known Mr. Stephens, who I took for an honeſt blunt man, I ſhould have thought only with horror of his ever being near my ſons, or in my houſe.

Going to the Conjuror's in Dean-ſtreet, was a great imprudence, as alſo was conſulting one three years before, on Ludgate-hill (I think it was) where I went with Mrs. Planta and Mrs. Pariſh, and alſo twice to a woman in Crown Court, once alone, and once with Mrs. Stephens : beſides this, I conſulted ſome Gypſies in a barn, three ſummers ago, at Paul's Walden, and three near there of different ſets.

C

I was

I was imprudent to carry my revenge, (as I then thought it) on the Planta family, fo far as to advife Mrs. Stephens to marry againft her confent, and to fend her off to Scotland, which I ought not to have done, even if fhe had been a good woman.

I had at this time a footman, one William Stamp, who (that I might not fo often appear to have letters from Mifs Graham) I ufed to fend now and then to Newcaftle, under pretence of feeing his brother who lived there (when I knew of a letter coming, which I often did before-hand) and bid him bring the letters to myfelf firft--- but this was all he knew of the matter.

It was not till after many months of conftant attention, and many marks of fincerity and friendfhip, that, juft as I was going to Paul's Walden for two months, (L. S.

(L. S. at Briftol) Mr. Gray ventured to give me fome verfes, which expreffed in a delicate, though rather in too tender a manner for mere friendfhip his, regard for me, and his great concern at my leaving London. From many circumftances, I had conceived fo high an opinion of the goodnefs of his heart and difpofition, that I was unwilling to lofe his friendfhip; fo that though I made no anfwer, I expreffed no anger, but continued correfponding with him openly and fairly till we both returned to town: foon after that, Lord S. went to Mr. Palgrave's, where he made fome ftay. One day juft after, as Mrs. Parifh and me were fitting at dinner, the poft brought me a letter from Mr. Lyon, in which he refufed, very uncivilly, to fend me a fmall fum of money, I told him I had written for by Lord S.'s directions;

and

and another letter from Mifs Graham, in which I found fhe had received a letter from her brother, who, as he began to do for fome time before, never fo much as mentioned me, but fpoke with the higheft commendations of a lady at Minorca, where he was arrived. As I was full of refentment at Mr. Lyon, and determined never more to think of Mr. James Graham, a fervant, (I don't recollect who, for I had no fecrets then) brought me a letter from Mr. Gray, who by an Enigma, very ingenioufly invented, had pitched upon that very day to fee how far he might venture: if I was angry, he might have explained it away; but if I underftood it, or pretended not to underftand it, then he might fpeak plainer. I chofe the latter method, and, full of refentment, thought I had revenged myfelf

on

on others, whilft I was literally on myfelf:
as I felt nothing for Mr. G. that exceeded
friendfhip, or gave me caufe to apprehend
the confequences of fuch a connection,
I confented to accept the love of a man,
whom I could always keep within bounds,
and whom I had conceived fuch an efteem
for, that I reckoned his friendfhip a comfort
I fhould be very forry to lofe. I faw him
three times when I knew Mrs. Parifh was
at the Mufeum, and met him for a fhort
time, as if by accident, at the Ring, without, I really believe, any fufpicion; but
as Lord S. was out of town---was expected foon to return, he preffed me to fee
him oftener at my houfe, and meet him
oftener at different places abroad; but this
was found impracticable without trufting
fomebody; and unfortunately, after taking
what we thought all neceffary precautions,

we

we agreed to truft George, whofe fecrecy and caution, we both thought we had 1ea-fon to be fatisfied with : we imprudently allowed him to tell us freely all the reports of the town, on every occafion, where either were in the leaft concerned.

He once, I am convinced, from fome interefted motive, rendered us a material fervice in preventing, by a ready turn, it's being detected that he was in the houfe. In this manner we went on till Lord S. re-turned to town, and he went to Bath, agreeing not to correfpond till I wrote to tell him he might return, which I did in a month's time, when Lord S. went away, but did not fee him for fome days, I can-not recollect how many, but once in that month he came up to town, and contrived to convey me a note, letting me know, that

his

his impatience had made him difobey my orders, and come up to town without a fummons, juft to fee me for an hour or two. He therefore begged I would meet him at Lever's, as by accident, which I did, and he returned directly to Bath, where he ftaid till I wrote to him to return. The weather being extremely fevere the day before he went to Bath, and I having met him very early in Saint James's Park, my fhoes extremely wet, and bottom of my petticoats, and I not having leifure to change them for fome time after I came home, I caught a flow fever, and cut myfelf dreadfully by falling on the ice; fo that I was ill when I went to Lever's, where I encreafed my complaints; and juft after Lord S. went away, I fell into an ague, in my face, from which I fuffered for near a month, half

of

of every twenty-four hours such torments, as nothing but the diforder I had juft after my marriage, can in any degree be compared to : my head fwelled fo, yet without eafing my pain, that I was blind, and even fpoke with pain. In this miferable condition, Mr. G. vifited me every evening unknown, as I thought by all but George, who let him in, and unfufpected by all but Mrs. Parifh, who fometimes remonftrated, but very gently, and I turned it off with a laugh or joke: at firft, fhe thought it only flirtation, and then fhe faid nothing ; for there is not, with all her pretended gravity and prudence, fo great a coquette, or one fo eafily flattered, even on her beauty, as fhe is; which, if you doubt, I can bring you many undeniable proofs. Witnefs for one thing, how

Alexan-

Alexander Nairne made her appear ridiculous.

I omitted to mention, in its proper place, that I told Mr. Gray he had my friendſhip and eſteem ; that my heart had long been in poſſeſſion of another, from whom I had determined to withdraw it, but had done it ſo ſhort a time, that I ſhould think it an injury againſt the friendſhip and confidence he was entitled to, if I concealed this circumſtance from him : alſo, that I had been ſo unhappy in matrimony, that I was determined never to engage myſelf indiſſolubly, though I would moſt faithfully, if, on theſe conditions, he would be ſatisfied with my affection, he ſhould have it entire if Lord S. died; that if he recovered, he muſt give me up; and that during my huſband's

life,

life, he muſt decline all thoughts of me. To all this with reluctance, and finding me peremptory, he conſented, and gave me his promiſe, which he ſtrictly kept till I was juſt recovered, when I found he expected to be rewarded, for the very great attentions (by writing to me all day, and fitting by me all the evening) which he conſtantly paid during my confinement: and one unfortunate evening I was off my guard, and ever after that (the middle of February) I lived occaſionally with him as his wife; and from that time, till my connection with you, I declare, I never had a thought of any other man.

I was once with child by him, before I heard of Lord S.'s death, which I did not till the 6th of April; but was ſo frightened and unhappy at it, that I prevailed on

him

him to bring me a quack medicine he had heard of for miscarriage, but never tried it: it was of a copperas substance, by the taste and look; he gave it me very reluctantly, as he said he did not know but it might be poison; however, I would have it.

All the time of my connection with Mr. Gray, precautions were taken; but an instant's neglect always destroyed them all: indeed, sometimes, even when I thought an accident scarce possible.

My folly was unpardonable, in trusting Mr. and Mrs. Stephens, George Stephens, Mr. Matra, Mr. Magra, Mr. Pemberton, (whom I once actually told I was married to Mr. Gray) and, above all things, George, in talking of my affairs and in-

D 2

tentions

tentions fo freely before them. I alfo
depended moft fatally on Mr. Peele's ho-
nefty; and, three or four times, added a
few lines in too free and jocofe a ftile to
Mr. Stephens, in the letters Mrs. Stephens
wrote him: he anfwered thefe paragraphs
in her letter, which fhe fhewed me. To
the beft of my recollection, I never wrote
to Mr. Stephens, but in his wife's letters,
which I read to her, or fhewed her, and
was added on the fame paper fhe wrote
on; and he never wrote to me any other
way; (all this was only whilft he was at
Winchefter, except once that he wrote only
to myfelf) having wrote to her the poft
before, which was a fulfome letter about
his wife, who, I told him, had not been
well, (which was true) owing, I believe,
to his abfence: and, I proteft, I thought
fo then.

This

This letter was chiefly, if not folely, expreffing his anxiety for her health, and dependance on my friendly care: I burnt this, with feveral other letters, a few days after I received it. This moment I recollect I have made a miftake; for I had a letter of thanks from him whilft he was on the expedition to Scotland. I had once a letter from Mr. G. Stephens, excufing himfelf from dining with me that day, according to invitation, as he was obliged to leave town on particular bufinefs. I correfponded conftantly with Mr. Pemberton for fome years ; and as he writes well, I have moft, if not all, his letters in London, (and the few I had from Captain Magra) at leaft, I had when I came down here laft; for I faw them amongft my papers when I came down to the election. All Dr. Brown's letters, feveral letters of

bufinefs

bufinefs to, and copies of letters from me, and fome others lefs material, were all removed before my return, and without my order. I wifh I had fome of Dr. Brown's letters; for they might have done me credit if feen.

When Mr. Stephens was at Winchefter, I advifed Mrs. Stephens to take a vomit, thinking fhe was with child; as I had taken a ridiculous notion into my head, that having children, made a man like his wife lefs.

According to Mifs Graham's defire and to prevent accidents, I burnt all th e letters I had from her as faft as they came; which I have fince repented of. I alfo burnt all Mr. Gray's letters from the fame fear: I mean only thofe which I received before

Lord

Lord Strathmore's return from Mr. Palgrave's.

I was always extremely filly, in not
minding reports; on the contrary, rather
encouraged them; partly, that I might
laugh at other people's abfurdities and
credulity, and partly, becaufe I left it to
time and reafon, to fhew they were falfe,
and thought a variety of reports would
puzzle people; fo that they would look
upon every one relating to me, as equally
falfe, and even not credit the truth.
Whereas, I have fince had reafon to fear it
had quite a contrary effect from what I
imagined and intended.

I foolifhly let George tell me all the ridiculous ftories he heard about Mr. Gray
and myfelf, and other people, fo far as
they

they related to us: and we ufed to laugh
at them; and as he was to have been our
courier, when we went abroad, which was
fixed for the 8th or 10th of April, to ftay
two, three, or more years; I ufed to let
him afk me any French words he did not
underftand, as he knew that language.
I gave him, the day or two before my
marriage, the deed drawn up on account
of my intended marriage with Mr. Gray,
along with a vaft heap of papers and letters, and an old leafe or two of the houfe,
of little cr no confequence, and bid him
put them all into the kitchen fire; but
before he could get there, called him
back, and after fwearing him to fecrefy,
bid him only burn the papers, and keep
the deed till I called for, or bid him burn,
it.

I declare

I declare folemnly, I did not do this from
any miftruft in your generofity or honour.
How could I? For I had a high opinion
of both, and had never feen or heard,
(except your behaviour to Mrs. Stoney,
which I believed to be only county of Dur-
ham malice) any thing which induced me
to think otherwife: befides, as I yielded
all my fortune without any referve for
myfelf, and as I am very far from an ex-
travagant woman, I never had a doubt,
you would chearfully fupply me with what
fums I might want, which would be very
fmall indeed after my debts were paid,
which I have often wifhed I could have
done before I married, Therefore, you
fee my doubt could by no means concern
myfelf: but it ftruck me, that having
taken fuch precautions on my children's

E   account,

account, (for whom I was anfwerable, though not for myfelf) with a man who I knew I could truft; I ought not to be lefs cautious with one whom I could not be fo ftrongly affured of: but I would not tell you of the paper, left it fhould look like miftruft.

Your fondnefs for my children, and the generofity I thought I difcovered in you, on all occafions, relating to pecuniary matters; together with the apparent open-nefs of your temper, which was very beara-ble till long after that, made me affure my-felf I had nothing to fear for my chil-dren, and reproach my heart, for ever having entertained a fhadow of a doubt. Therefore, before we came to the elec-tion, I ordered George to burn the paper; and

and when we were at Gibfide, I once afked him if he had; and he declared he had: but not content with that, I had written three or four lines in French, when I told him, (not having time to tell him when I fpoke to him) that I charged him never to reveal having had that deed, or of any other thing he knew relating to me; and threatened him if he did. This was madnefs, and thank God I changed my mind and burnt the paper, (for whilft I hefitated, I believe he went away) elfe he might have fhewn that paper to Mr. Lyon: fo chance ftood my friend, I confefs, and not prudence.

I told you, if I don't greatly miftake or forget, that I gave Mr. Stephens 1000l. within a month or fix weeks before my marriage with you, but that I could not fpeak

certainly

certainly as to the time. I have fince re-
collected that I told you wrong. About
that time, I gave Mrs. Stephens a fum for
her own ufe, of 5ol. or 1ool. (I cannot be
pofitive which, but I think the latter) and
this muft have been what mifled me.——
Something you faid fince you came to
Gibfide—I think it was his being fo com-
municative, and fpeaking his opinion fo
blunt to every body—reminded me of the
miftake I had made : would I had told
you of it then ; but I foolifhly, out of
fear of your anger, delayed telling you
till new : It was the very evening of the
day I was married, that I gave Mrs. Stephens, and not Mr. Stephens, the 1ool.
which I defired fhe would accept for her-
felf and him, in performance of a promife I had made him the day (the fift I
ever faw him) before he went off with
that

that more than woman, that I would pay his debts; he having told me at that time, which I remember greatly prejudiced me in his favour, that he had debts to the amount of some hundred pounds, and that he could not be eafy in his mind, if he entered into an engagement with Mrs. Stephens; and therefore lived in my family (as I told him he was to do) without letting us know how he was fituated. This, together with the affection he took that opportunity of expreffing for his laft wife, made me rejoice in having met with fuch a perfon. I told him, if he made Mrs. Stephens a good hufband, and behaved in the manner I had no doubt he would, I would take care he fhould have no trouble from his debts—I really believe he made her a good hufband, (I ftill believe he does a better than fhe deferves, I am

fure

fure he cannot a worfe) and I gave her, the evening of the day I married you, 1000l. to give him, doubting not that would be a pleafing ftep to both, and endear her more to him. His apparent fincerity and honeft freedom in expoftulating with me, when I told him I was married to you, pleafed and affected me greatly, and moved me to a fincere forrow and penitence. I thought it became a Clergyman and an honeft one, and I thought him fincere and honeft in what he faid, and that he rifked his fortune to fpeak truth: even when him and his wife went to France, I actually thought them—to that very time, but no longer, from fome hints you directly after that let drop—fincere and faithful friends to both you and me, and grieved you did not treat them better; fuch was my infatuation. May Mr. S.

forgive

forgive me, the fad wretch I unknowingly gave him.

It was the night, or two nights after this; the night Mrs. S. and Mrs. G. S. came from Paul's Walden, that I fat up with Mr. George Stephens till two o'clock (I think it was) in the morning, which gave you fuch offence. Our whole converfation was about you; he was of a different opinion from his brother, who he faid thought and fpoke like a Parfon, but not like a gentleman of unprejudiced education; a man of nice honour and delicate feelings. He commended what I had done, which he faid he never fhould have doubted my doing, had he not believed I was previoufly married. He commended me much, and blamed Mr. Gray. This, and obfervations and ac-

counts

counts of what happened at Paul's Walden, was the whole purport of our converfation that night, which was the only particular, or fo circumftantial one, I ever had with him in my life.

As to Mr. Stephens, I believe it is needlefs to tell you, I never faw him before Mr. Matra introduced him to me; and Mr. Matra was introduced by the commendation of his brother, the Captain, and by the very ftrong ones of Dr. Solander.

As to Mrs. Parifh, fhe provoked me by an uninterrupted feries of ill-temper, deceit, felf-intereftednefs, and ingratitude; with obftinacy, and in many refpects a bad method with my children; and I found fhe mifled and mis-informed me in the objects of my charity; in short, she was too insufferable, else I would have retained her. But as I owe her nothing, and she much to me, I shall say no more about her.

I cannot be positive as to the month, but think it must have been in October, when I went to the Conjuror in Pear-street. Mrs. Stephens, Mr. Pennick, Mr. Matra (all of whom I think breakfasted with me that morning) were of the party, and Capt. Magra met us, I think half way. Mrs. Stephens told me of a Conjuror at the Old Bailey, who she had been to; and I had a curiosity to see him. Accordingly, we walked to the Old Bailey, where we met a little boy, who came up to us and asked if we wanted the gentleman who so many people came after, and that he

F would

would conduct us to him? we faid yes,
and he carried us through blind alleys to
Pear-ftreet: Mrs. Stephens told me afterwards it was not the man fhe had been to
before. It was between 11 and 12, as
near as I can recollect, when we got to
Pear-ftreet, and there were fuch a number of people in the room we waited in,
to whom the Conjuror was firft engaged,
and they took fo long a time to have their
fortunes told, that it was almoft 6 o'clock
before they began with us; and Capt.
Magra and felf were weak enough to go
down twice to the cellar or room below
ftairs, where he fat. Capt. Magra, who
went down in perfect unbelief, came up
convinced of the man's knowledge from
what he told him. The two brothers, Mrs. Stephens, Mr. Pennick, and
myfelf, returned in a hackney-coach,

which

which was called in Smithfield, from Pear-ftreet to Grofvenor-fquare, or very near it, I forgot which; and I did not get home till paft eight o'clock, almoft ftarved to death with cold and hunger; for it was with great difficulty we procured, a little before we came away, a little bad bread and water, and two logs of green wood, which we put in a chimney-place where there was no grate, and which gave very little warmth, in a cold rainy day, to the coldeft room I ever was in, and which had no other furniture than two (or three at moft) rotten chairs, and a wooden trunk. I went by the name of the widow Smith, and Mrs. Stephens, and Mr. Pennick, by fome other, which I cannot at prefent recollect, though I have endeavoured to do it. During the firft part of the time we were waiting, Mr.

F 2

Pennick

Pennick wrote fome verfes (and repeated feveral quotations) which begun with,

" Thro' Dirty-ftreet we bent our way,
" To have our Fortunes told to-day (or this day.")

To the beft of my recollection there were eight or ten more of the fame fort of lines followed thefe, but of which I could not for my life recollect one word, any more than of two or four (I believe four) lines I wrote likewife on the partition, which contained fome reflection on a general head; to the beft of my remembrance, it was againft matrimony; I am fure, at leaft I think I am, that I fhould recollect them if I faw them again, and I would tell you. Before we went away, we rubbed all the verfes out with our fingers fo carefully, that I can fwear that none but the two which you fhewed me

were

were poffibly legible, and they not without the greateft difficulty, the pencil being
blacker as they were firft written, I fup-
pofe was the reafon they were plainer.
Mr. Magra, and I think Mr. Pennick, ftaid
fupper; and I believe it was nearer one
than twelve when they went away: I cannot recolleft whether Mr. Gray fupped
with me that night, but I know he did
not dine in Grofvenor-fquare. Mrs. Stephens fung and played from dinner till
fupper, and afterwards we laughed at the
adventures of the day. When we were
at the Conjuror's waiting, a variety of
ftrange citizens, &c. came in and out, as
there was but one anti-chamber for us
all: the gentlemen entered into converfation with them all, but I only fpoke to
two; the firft a woman, the beft and moft
decent looking, who told me her hiftory,

and

and her repenting of not taking the Conjuror's advice, who she consulted two or three times, or oftener, in a year. I passed myself upon her for a Grocer's widow, and was come to consult the Conjuror, whether I should marry a Brewer, or Sugar-boiler, who proposed to me amongst others, and I had ten children. Mrs. Stephens also spoke, the only one I think she did. The other person I spoke to, was a little Portuguese Jew, about 15 years old, whose father, a rich broker or pawnbroker, Capt. Magra knew; and we two spoke to him in Spanish, though not much: his father had sent him to find out who stole some of his silver spoons. It is impossible a more exact or true account of this silly affair can be given, than is now before you.

In

In the courfe of this long ftory, three or four trifling circumftances efcaped my memory, fo that I cannot place them under the proper heads they belonged to, and now they will appear totally unconnected; but as I profefs (and moft fincerely) to omit not one circumftance, either material or trifling, and that is the only merit I pretend or wifh for in this Narration; I fhall attend to exactnefs, and not regularity, which you will perceive I have all along too much neglected, having written things exactly as they prefented themfelves to my memory.

When Mr. Scot gave me the blue ring, I gave him one my father had given me, exactly the fame, by which means nobody perceived I had got a new ring, and this none knew but ourfelves. I endeavoured

to

to perfuade Mr. Liddle, by hints, &c. it was the Duke of Buccleugh and not his brother, whom I had a liking for, and puzzled him, that he fometimes thought the Duke, and fometimes Mr. Scot.

When I went to the Park, Kenfington Gardens, or any way in the ftreet to meet Mr. Gray, I forgot to mention that George walked behind me, and therefore knew of it; alfo when I went to the Gypfies and Conjuror's.

When I mentioned William Stamp, I likewife forgot to tell you that twice or thrice, in paying him a bill, I gave him fome money (a guinea or two at moft) over what was due, under pretence of rewarding his diligence as a fervant, but, in fact, as a bribe (though I did

not

not tell him fo) not to fpeak of the letters he brought, as I told you, from Newcaftle.

N B. It had almoft flipt my memory to tell you that Lord S.'s beauty, which was then very great, and a dream or rather vifion, to which I was foolifh enough to give more credit than it deferved, were two great inducements to me to marry Lord S.

One thing more, and I have quite done. I do affure you, you did me great injuftice in thinking thofe fits were affected to which I have fo many years been fubjeft, and from which I have fuffered fo much at various times. The laft I had, alfo the night before Dr. Scott left Gibfide, was indeed real; but I confefs, that out

G   of

of fulkinefs for what you had faid to me that day, I did not fpeak or anfwer you fo foon as I was able.

I have now punctually, minutely, and moft entirely given you a full account of every thing I ever did, faid, or thought, that was wrong.

I have, under my own hand, furnifhed you with a perpetual fund for unkindnefs, and even good excufe for bad ufage ; but you are my hufband—I obey you, and if you continue to diftruft, abufe, and think of me as you have hitherto done, Providence muft and will decide which of us two is moft to blame.

I know, according to your promife, you will never again repeat paft griev-
ances ;

ances; but if you think of them I shall suffer as much and more from the unkindness, your brooding silently over them will constantly create; for indeed I fear you are of an unforgiving, and in this respect, unforgetting temper; else you could not, for so many months together, have behaved so uniformly cruel to one whose whole wish and study was to please you.

If you think my sincerity and unreserved confession of my faults may entitle me to ask a favour, let me beg your promise to burn these papers, at least, that you will destroy them when I die, that I may not stand condemned and disgraced, under my own hand, to posterity.

I am going to fulfil my promise of laying before you all the crimes and foibles of my life. To prove that I am sincere,

I know

I know not what method to take. I cannot make any imprecations on myself, as I am already so loaded with misery that there is only one curse which is not mine already. Therefore, I only wish that one may happen to me, if I do not speak (without the least extenuation) the whole and exact truth: that I do this I can only refer to a long series of sufferings and patience to prove, if it please God to give me strength and resolution to trail out my existence till even you are convinced, by my example, that a person who has once been vicious, may repent and become good.

I am convinced that the want of a proper sense of religion has been the original cause of all my errors; all the grounds of this mischief was laid before my father died, and then I was only between eleven

and

and twelve years old. My father was the youngeſt of four ſons, and intended for a profeſſion, but never would give his mind in the leaſt to ſtudy; on the contrary, when only eighteen he ran away, and laid out what money his mother had given him for other purpoſes, in buying a com- miſſion in the army, where he continued till he came to the eſtate. As he was uncommonly handſome, and a great rake in his youth, he grew very pious in his advanced years, and having felt the want of education and ſtudy, for he was (as I have heard him ſay determined his heir ſhould not feel the ſame inconveniences; accord- ingly, he brought me up with a view to my being as accompliſhed at thirteen, as his favourite firſt wife was at that age, in every kind of learning, except Latin

At

At four years old I could read uncommonly well, and was kept tight to it, made to get many things off by heart. I read the Bible, but at the same time equal or greater pains were taken to inſtruct me in the Mythology of every Heathen nation that ever exiſted; and my father, who was a real patriot and a brave man, was continually expatiating on the patriotic virtues, and ſhining merits of the ancient philoſophers and heroes. My mind was ſo puzzled with ſuch a variety of religions, that, except the firm belief of a God, I knew not which of all the modes of worſhip to adopt from real conviction; as to the weak judgment of a child, all appeared equally ſupported by trádition. However, I ſaw my father was a chriſtian, and a proteſtant, therefore I called and believed myſelf one too, though it is not

till

ill within thefe few months that I have
had leifure, compofure, and inclination to
inveftigate thefe matters ; and now I am
become a chriftian from conviction.

Another misfortune for me, was, that
though my father did not applaud fuicide
and revenge in general terms, by their
names ; I have often heard him fpeak
highly of men who have been guilty of
them ; Cato for one inftance. My father's
whole care and attention was beftowed on
the improvement of my knowledge, in
whatever I fhewed a genius for ; and in
acquiring me a great ftock of health,
hardening and ftrengthening my confti-
tution by every poffible means, often the
moft rigid ones. My father was continually talking of, and endeavouring to incul-
cate into me, fentiments of generofity;
grati-

gratitude, fortitude, and duty to himfelf, and an infatiable thirſt for all kinds of knowledge. But I never heard him once ſay, to the beſt of my recollection, that chaſtity, patience, and forgiveneſs of injuries, were virtues; and he was very paſſionate. During his life, my mother did not interfere with my education. When I was between eleven or twelve years old, he died. Amongſt other things, my father made me ſpeak ſpeeches before much company, and get moſt part of Ovid's Metamorphoſes by heart, as well as Milton, &c. My mother ſtaid at Gib-ſide, where my father died, till I was near thirteen. We went then to London and ſtaid till I was fourteen, ſhe continuing all that time in ſuch affliction, as to be incapable of attending either to my education or mo-rals: for the former ſhe relied on the beſt

maſter,

master, and my own defire of learning, and for my conduct, fhe relied on an old maiden aunt, Mrs. J. B. who came up to town, and till I married I lived chiefly with her. This woman firft introduced me into the world, when my mother could not go out. She had been a celebrated beauty, and extremely vain; but, unfortunately for me, of nothing more, than having a niece who was one of the greateft fortunes in England; and (though I ought not to fay it, nor do I but with confufion and fhame, that I did not employ my talents better) a prodigy of learning. Mrs. Montague, amongft others, was pleafed to honour me with her friendfhip, approbation, and correfpondence, (I can yet fhew feveral of her letters) and this continued without interruption till Lord S. after my marriage, obliged me to break off with her, in a

H   very

very rude and abrupt manner, (going no more to her Sundays, and only once a year rapping at her door) telling me she was a wild, light, silly woman, of bad character, and not fit for my acquaintance. Sadly against my inclination, I was forced to comply, and give her up, with many others.

But, to return to my aunt. she was for two years (after which I returned under my mother's care) so indulgent a chaperon, that I must say, if I had not been more prudent than most young girls of my age, I might have been less so.

The first imprudence I ever was guilty of, was carrying on for twelve months a flirtation with Mr. Scott, the Duke of Buccleugh's brother, whom I frequently met

and

and danced with at children's balls, as they were called, and chiefly at the Duchefs of Northumberland's. Girls and boys were admitted from five or fix, to fourteen or fifteen years old. I was thirteen when this began, and Mr. Scott was a year or two older, I cannot be fure which. He liked my converfation, and as he was fmart and clever, I liked his; and all this would have only been a flirtation, I really believe, had not my filly coufin, Liddell, who was his fchool-fellow, and was ftaying with my mother, teazed us into a belief that we were in love with each other; however, no further engagement paffed between us, than that he told me he had a tender affection for me, and liked my company better than any other girl's; at which I was not difpleafed, but in return, I particularly remember I made ufe of the words, " ten-

der

der efteem for him." He went foon
after into the army, and before he fet out
for Germany afked me to exchange rings
with him, which I readily agreed to ; and
you know and have often feen the ring.
He died about a twelve month after he
went abroad, of the fmall pox, in the natural way.

N. B. The prefent Mr. Charles Fox had
a great liking for me, and followed me,
but had too much pride to tell me fo directly, as he faw I preferred Mr. Scott, for
which reafon, I know, he abufed both.

This affair of Scott's, was a great imprudence, but, thank God, no worfe.

After I recovered the fhock of Mr.
Scott's death, whofe mother, Lady Dal-
keith, hurt me much by her unfeeling-
nefs; I amufed myfelf, till I engaged to

marry

marry Lord S. with alternate ftudy and di-
verfions; fuch as public places, &c. I
had, I do affure you, no partiality for any
man in the world, though I had a great
many offers made to my mother for me;
as I told every body who offered, that I
fhould not hear any thing on that fubject
from any perfon, as all offers of that
kind muft come through my mother: accordingly, they all found themfelves obliged to apply to her; by which conduct,
I was both efteemed an uncommon prudent girl, and had the fatisfaction of refufing a great many people of rank, in
fuch due form as flattered my vanity, and
made it impoffible they could deny (as
they might otherwife) that they had offered to me. And fo great was my repu-
tation for prudence in thefe refpects, that
though a young Venetian Marquis, with

my

my mother's acknowledged confent and approbation, attended on me for near a twelve month, to all public places as Cicefbeo, and was frequent in his vifits at our houfe, the world did us juftice in believing this connection was entirely owing to my mother; and wifhing me to be perfect in the Italian language, and to his fpeaking Englifh fo very badly, that he could keep no company, but fuch as fpoke Italian (for his French was little better) and the number of thofe was ftill much more inconfiderable at that period than it is now, efpecially amongft the ladies. My mother was always partial to the Italian nation and their language. The Marquis, who was on his travels through Europe, proceeded to Paris, and fo we parted with the fame civility and indifference as we met: he fent my two little dogs from Paris;

wrote

wrote once or twice from France, and once from Peterſburgh; ſince when, I have heard nothing of or from him.

I gave ſome encouragement to Lord Strathmore, but it was ſlight, though more than to others: he wrote a letter to me with a declaration; and having, as I afterwards found, tried unſuccefsfully, many ways to get it conveyed to me, ſent it by Mrs. Baker, who came under a pretence of ſpending a day or two with my mother, who, at that time, hated the ſight of her, and never aſked her to ſtay all night, as ſhe thought her very officious, in ſpeaking much, and greatly, in praiſe of the Lord Strathmore's family; as my mother thought, (though ſhe never poſitively told me ſo) I ſhewed more partiality to Lord S. than to any other perſon. Mrs. Baker took

an

an opportunity, when she was out of the room, to give me Lord S.'s letter; I guessed what it was, but, after reading a few of the first lines, returned it to Mrs. B. telling her, I would not receive any letters in that manner, and I thought the office she had undertaken very unbecoming of her, or any gentlewoman; and that the gentleman, whose name I had not looked at, or was desirous to know, (here she interrupted me and said it was Lord S.) must apply to my mother, if he meant to have any answer. I then left her under great mortification; but I did not tell my mother what had passed, from an apprehension, that it might set her more against my marrying Lord S.; and, because she was so reserved, that she did not treat even me, with the confidence, I think, a daughter entitled to. Therefore, I never durst open

my

my heart to, or confult upon thefe fub-
jects ; and to this I attribute, in a great
meafure, the chief of my misfortunes
through life. Indeed, I muft fay, I was
always a dutiful child to her, till I was
married, and I have often heard her
own it.

Soon after Lord S. received my anfwer
from Mrs. Baker, he came to Gibfide, and
made his propofals in form to my mother,
who told him, fhe would acquaint me,
and as we were going directly to London,
for which place he alfo was going to fet
out, he fhould have his anfwer there : but
fhe did not tell me of his having offered,
till two days after he had left the houfe ;
and then affected to mention it as a thing
fhe did not doubt I fhould refufe ; as, fhe
faid, there were three objections: diforder

I   in

in the family; a mother, and many brothers and fifters, whom, perhaps, I fhould find troublefome; and, laftly, (the chief with her) his being a Scotchman. The firft, I had often heard, was only a falfe report, and believed fincerely it proceeded from envy, ill nature, and partly fpite. the fecond, would afford me an opportunity of endearing myfelf to my hufband, whofe relations, I never doubted, would behave well to me; and the third, was a recommendation, as I had always a much greater partiality for the Scotch and Irifh, than for the Englifh.

I accordingly told her, that I had no objection to Lord Strathmore; but, that if her's were infuperable, I would not marry without her confent— only claimed the privilege of not marrying at all; which,

which, in that cafe, I was determined on. She then gave her confent, and faid, fhe would tell Lord S. when he came to town, as agreed on; and we went to town directly. I muft not omit here to mention, that Mrs. Parifh, then my governefs, fpoke greatly againft Lord S.

His favourite uncle, Charles Lyon, taking a fever, and dying juft after we left the country, detained Lord S. fo long from coming up to London to receive this, and as he durft not write, I did not know the caufe, that I thought myfelf flighted. Though grieved and provoked, I put on a cheerful countenance, and danced frequently at Almack's, with various people who followed me, though they had not then declared themfelves: amongft thefe, the moft affiduous were

Lord

Lord Mountſtuart and Mr. Chaloner. I
gave neither of them encouragement; yet
they contrived one night to quarrel, and
put the whole room in an uproar at Almack's, about who ſhould ſit next me at
ſupper. Both went out in a paſſion; a
challenge was given, but prevented by one
of the gentlemen (I believe Mr. Chaloner,
but never could be ſure which) aſking par-
don. Lady Mountſtuart, then Miſs Wind-
for, ſat one ſide of me, and having even
then a partiality for Lord M.S. begged me to
take notice of and encourage him, as he
was like a madman, and expoſed himſelf
to all the company. I confeſs, I did, with
a premeditated deſign, ſhew great civility
to Lady Bute and her daughters, one night
at Almack's, in order, that before Lord S.
arrived, and my engagement to him was
known, I might have an opportunity of

refuſing

refuling Lord M. S. This civility, which
Lady Bute conftrued into encouragement,
had the defired effect; and over-reached
her great caution and pride (which I knew
fhe had) in not offering, with a chance
of her fon's being refuled : next morning
fhe waited on my mother, to propofe for
her fon, and met a mortification which
hurt her much, and made him keep his
bed for a week. This I confefs, was down-
right girlifhnefs, mifchievoufnefs, and vanity.

My marriage-treaty with Lord S. for
one delay or other, trailed on about a year
and a half ; during which, I found our
tempers, difpofitions, and turns different
—wifhed to retract (and would, if I durft
have confulted with my mother) but my
pride, and fome times my weaknefs, would

not

not let me · at length we were married, at Paul's Walden, and I was brought a fortnight after to Gibfide ; though I had began to be ill, juft before I fet out, as two or three of the party had fluxes at Paul's Walden ; which we attributed to my mother's bad Port-wine. I faid, though I never tafted but one glafs of it, that it had alfo affected me, in a moft dangerous and poifonous manner, by a partial erup-tion ; though I don't believe the doctors were, or could be, impofed upon.

I intended candidly, and in the fulleft manner, to lay before you every action of my life, relative to the leaft imprudence I ever was guilty of. I have written a good deal'; but as you are impatient, and per-ceiving I labour under a load of imputa-tions, yet unknown to me, though cre-

dited

dited by you, many of which, I dare fay,
are falfe; I fhall, till after this is finifhed,
leave the tiifling things, which were only
inadvertencies any gul might be and is
guilty of; and haften to tell you, in as
few words as poffible, every imprudence,
and every crime, I have been guilty of,
fince my marriage with Lord Strathmore,
which is as far back as I imagine you are
immediately anxious to know.

I had by him all my five children; and
during that time, never had one thought,
did one action, or faid one word, which
Heaven might not know without blaming
me, or indeed himfelf; except the dif-
like I had but too much caufe to entertain for Mr. Lyon. Before I had been
many months married, however, I put up
with that, and the difagreeable behaviour

of

of the reft of the family, and concealed it as much as poffible from the world, till he publicly, and caufelefsly, as many can witnefs, infulted me in the public rooms at Edinburgh, where I was with him and Mrs. Lyon, who was juft married, all the race-week without Lord Strathmore; during which time, he behaved in fuch a manner, as fcandalized the whole town of Edinburgh; who, at that time, hated him as much as they liked and pitied me. I complained mildly to Lord Strathmore about his brother; but it was an unfortunate and moft prejudiced rule with him, that Mr. Lyon could not err; fo I got no other redrefs than his faying, that though he was hafty, he had a good heart, and never meant to offend. I never complained to my mother on any occafion of Lord S or his family; but on the contrary,

trary, expreffed an uncommon regard for both, of which fhe was jealous, and made her believe they ufed me extremely well. for as I had married him againft her advice, my pride would not let me complain, had they ufed me ten times worfe.

The year before this, Mr. Robert Graham, of Fuitry, took all opportunities to be in my company, and to exprefs, though not improperly, his regard and attention to me. He once told me fo pofitively, and received fuch an anfwer as was proper, and which, from my foolifh flirting with him, I dare fay he did not expect. He went from Glames in a pet, and being a man of violent refentments (which in all inftances have turned out againft himfelf, he directly propofed to Mifs Peggy Mylne, who always had a penchant for him; but

K whom

whom he had taken every opportunity, both in public and private, to abufe in a moft groundlefs and violent manner; and to profefs, that he would rather die than marry her. yet fhe confented—they were married fuddenly without his parents con-fent.

The year before, when I was on a vifit to his mother, I faw for the firft time, and not again for two years, his youngeft brother, James: he was quite a boy, but a very extraordinary one, and I muft con-fefs, much too forward for his years, and too confcious of thofe fhining talents, which no heart can, in fome degree with-out difficulty, be proof againft, when he chofe to exert his art. I have the greateft reafon to think, he, from that't'me, form-ed a defign of enjoying my affections : he

made

made many attempts to come with his other brothers to Glamis; but they conftantly, as Mifs Graham told me, refufed to bring him: and he introduced himfelf, or rather in a manner forced himfelf in, to come to Glamis one day with his fifter; when fhe walked to Bridge Town, fcarce three miles from Glamis, where fhe, and indeed myfelf, often ufed to go, to fee an amiable and elegant woman, one Mrs. Douglas, wife to my dear Emilia's brother; where he fometimes, and particularly at that time, was ftaying. He, as I afterwards found, offered to fet her home to Glamis, when fhe was ftaying with me, but fhe would not let him; upon which he told her, there were droves of horned cattle on the road, as it was the high road to Forfar, where he told her it was market-day; and knowing her extreme timi-

dity

dity in that refpect, he was fure fhe would
not refufe him. She did not, and as he
has a confummate affurance and high opinion of himfelf, though he fometimes
affects modefty, he introduced himfelf to
Lord S. and me; and under one pretence
or other, contrived to ftay a fortnight at
Glamis; during which time, he did every
thing to ingratiate himfelf, and fucceed-
ed fo well, that he could not help per-
ceiving the progrefs he had made. and
indeed, when he preffed me to it, I partly confeffed it. Luckily his fifter was
ftaying with me; fo we never were alone,
but us three walking a whole morning,
to the amount of feveral miles meafured,
in the great hall at Glamis; every turn
he marked with a pencil. I had my hand
on a piece of paper he pinned up at the
end of the hall, which paper and pencil,
unluckily

unluckily a very remarkable one, he told me he would preferve as his life; but I hope he has loft it. I am not fure, but I have reafon to think, he got fome of my hair from his fifter. He was ordered to London to join his regiment.

Mr Graham, of Fuitry, did not know of my liking for his brother; but as his affiftance was abfolutely neceffary in getting the money conveyed to London, which I was bent on fending him as from an unknown; Mifs G. told him that, out of friendfhip for her, and thinking her brother James a very promifing young man, I meant to fend him fome money to fpend in London: accordingly, he affifted her in forwarding it to him. Mifs Graham contrived a way for us to correfpond, which, though the letters were intercepted,

tercepted, nothing could be difcovered, as we fixed initials quite different from the real names; by which we fignified our-felves, and the people we had ofteneft occafion to mention : and when I meant to tell her any thing, or fhe to me, always faid C. L. bid me tell A. B. fo and fo. I burnt all her letters as I received them, which I am now forry I did, and I de-manded the fame of her; but fhe beg-ged of me earneftly to let her keep, for her perufal and entertainment, fometimes thofe parts of my letters which did not con-cern her brother:—that, I would not refufe her, promifing me fhe would burn or deface every word concerning him, and fhewing me a letter for an example of what fhe faid.

I faw

I faw Mr. James Graham in London after he left Scotland, juft before he failed for Minorca; but found him much altered towards me, and therefore my pride made me treat him with the indifference I ought, though it almoft broke my heart. This is all, and far too much, of this foolifh affair.

I had almoft forgotten to mention, that Mifs Graham told me, the fecond of her three brothers (David) was a great admirer of mine, and perpetually talking of me; and that when he did, his eyes ufed to dart fire, and fparkle like diamonds (thefe were her very words) but I had only her word for thinking he had any partiality for me. He was ftill handfomer than either of his brothers (my favourite was the leaft fo) but before I was fcarce

acquainted

acquainted with David, I was fo taken up with James, that I paid no attention to him. James has or had a picture of me, which he drew himfelf from memory; and I am told by the few who faw it, that it refembles me more than any picture which was ever taken of me. I ought to tell you, why I faid Mrs. G. was not good and virtuous. I am convinced, fhe did Mifs Douglas's (Emelia) memory a great injuftice, and in a moft treacherous manner; for I am fure it fprang from her. She then quarrelled with Mrs. Mylne, an amiable woman, and univerfally refpected, becaufe her eldeft brother married her fecond daughter; an agreeable good girl, but with no fortune: and before this, fhe ufed to profefs juft the fame friendfhip and difinterefted friendfhip fhe afterwards did for me; which

had

had she been a man, was seemingly so
violent, I should have called it love. She
was very deceitful and cunning, and, I
believe, had an intrigue with Mr. Demp-
ster: she would with Mr. Nairn, had he
chosen.

I asked Mr. and Mrs. Stephens, at the
same time, for some of their hair (I think
they were together, but of that cannot be
positive) when I asked them. I asked also,
Mr. Matra for a lock of his. Mr. Stephens had a ring composed, half of Mrs.
Stephens's hair and half of mine; it is
quite plain, not set round with any thing:
I cannot be certain whether I gave it him,
or whether he got it himself—I think I
gave it him myself; it was immediately
after his marriage: but what puzzles my
positive recollection is, that I know about

L   that

that time, Mrs. Stephens afked me for some of my hair, which I gave her. She told me, foon after, that fhe intended giving George Walker fome prefent, for the trouble he had about Mr. —— and her letters ; and that fhe intended giving him a breaft locket, with her own hair fet in one part of it, and a bit of mine with it, and that fhe had fome of it by her ; which, as fhe could not afford to make him a great prefent of intrinfic value, fhe thought nothing could be more acceptable to fo faithful a fervant. I told her, as I then thought, that he certainly was fo, and had been of great ufe to Mr. G. and me ; but, that I thought it an odd prefent, thefe were my very words ; and as I faid no more, fhe befpoke it, and when it was finifhed, the addition of the piece of hair, which was very fmall and

covered

covered with glafs, prevented its faften-
ing: fo it was returned, and Mrs. Stephens got one ready made at a pawnbroker's fhop, one day when fhe and me walked into the city, out of curiofity to fee
thofe kind of fhops, and called at a great
number: at one of them, I bought a watch
which I gave George.—I gave George,
about this time, fome very old horfe furniture; which, though quite fpoilt, befides being infinitely too antiquated for ufe,
contained fo much filver, that if I do not
miftake, it fold for upwards of 20l.: Mrs
Parifh had difpleafed me fo much, and, apt
as I am to be impofed on, had fhewn fuch
proofs of a dirty interestednefs, that I determined to part with her; but, as fhe had
lived with, and partly educated me fo
many years, was refolved it fhould be on
good terms; therefore, I refolved to raife

L 2

2000l.

2000l. by any means, the firſt money I ex-
pended. This, I thought, would be ſuf-
ficient to make her eaſy in circumſtances,
if ſhe was intereſted as I thought her, or,
if it was poſſible I had been miſtaken in
her character, convince me by her ſtill re-
maining with me, that I had done her in-
juſtice. This I concealed from my mother, till I put it in execution, being greatly diſpleaſed at her offer of lending me
500l. when ſhe knew, what diſtreſs I
was in, and that ſuch a ſum would
do nothing for me. I even denied to
my mother, when I gave Mrs. Pariſh
the 2000l. (which I did at Paul's Walden,
borrowing it of Mr. Peele, when he came
there after Lord S.'s death, ſome time before I returned to town) and my mother
believed I did not entertain the moſt dif-
tant

tant thought that she would leave me, except by marrying.

As Mrs. Parish's conduct to me, has
been, her sister's excepted, the most vile,
ungrateful, and pernicious, that ever was
heard of; I shall say nothing about it here,
as, during the whole, I cannot tax myself
with doing any thing wrong; and this paper is only meant as a confession of my
crimes and faults. But, if you please, I will
tell you every circumstance relating to her
behaviour, and to the strange manner
she behaved to Mr. G. when, at his earn-
est request, he thinking she might be of
use to me, I consented to his talking to
her, and attempting to persuade her to stay
with me, as from himself.

Just

Juſt before ſhe left me, I went to Paul's Walden, to tell my mother I was married, that I might get the ſtart of Mrs. Pariſh, who, I was ſure, would write to tell her the very day after our parting was agreed on; and who, I believe, had it not been for intereſted motives, and the fear of diſpleaſing my mother, would have told her long before, which I have many reaſons to be certain ſhe did not. I did not intend to declare my marriage till April, juſt before we left England, or to be married actually till we were abroad, a ſhort time before I laid in; and I propoſed to ſtay three or four years to viſit France, Italy, Hungary, and Bohemia, and perhaps Spain and Portugal: I did not tell even Mr. Gray, poſitively, my deſigns about marriage.

But

But I had almoft forgotten, that the reafon why I mentioned the 2000l. and Mrs.
Parifh, was, that I might tell you, foon
after I came out of town after Loid S.'s
death, I was perpetually fending George
backwaids and forwards to London, to
raife the 2000l. After I applied to Mr.
Mayne, (who faid, he could not lend me
that fum without his partner's concur-
rence), I then applied to Fernandez, and
a number of other Jews, who did not
know me, and I did not fign my name to
the letter; but they would not lend me
on any other terms than annuities, which
I would not think of, and they were
dreadfully unreafonable ones. If I could,
I would have raifed three thoufand pounds,
to have had one thoufand pounds in hand.
When George went backwards and for-

wards

wards to thefe Jews, I ufed always to write to, and hear from Mr. G. who ftayed juft about that time after me in town. When I was at Paul's Walden, and he in Scotland, all his letters to me came under cover to George, and he always directed mine to him; and under fome pretence or other, went to Welwyn, Stephenage, Hitchin, or Hatfield, and put them in himfelf.

When I came occafionally to Paul's Walden, for a week or a few days, once or twice a fortnight, after I was fettled in town, I ufed to enclofe my letters often, under cover to George, (whom, on that account, I generally left in town) and with it, directions fometimes to him, to fend meffages, or deliver notes about plays, operas, dinings, tea-drinking, &c. and

often

often inclofed directions to the houfe-keeper of affairs relating to the houfe, &c. and fometimes I enclofed to George under the frank to her, and bid her give it once or twice. I remember, that having enclofed a number of letters and notes to be delivered out, I faid, Go and tell Mr. G. I have no time to write now, but fhall be in Grofvenor-fquare, and expect him at fuch an hour. When Mrs. Stephens eloped, and I came to Paul's Walden, I left George in town to receive the Planta family, and fend me a conftant account of their motions; which he did: I wifh I had kept them, as you might have liked to fee them; but being, as I thought, of no confequence after fhe returned and knew the accounts, I burnt them.

M

Mr. Mylne, whofe fifter married Mr. G. only lent Lord S. 10,000l. the half of what he is worth ; and though the phyficians declared her life was in danger, if fhe did not go to Italy for her health directly (where I believe fhe now is) he was threatened to be ftopped by Lord S.'s creditors, who would come upon him. In this fituation, he defired Mr. G. when he faw him in Scotland, and who he knew had long been an acquaintance of mine, to write to me, and beg I would allow him to ufe my name, and fay, I would fee the money fhould be paid out of the Scotch eftates, and the firft debt difcharged. Mr. G. told him, he could not poffibly take fuch a liberty with me ; efpecially as he had not written to me even a letter of condolence, as civility required, fince Lord S.'s death. But Mr. Mylne

preffed

preffed him fo much, and conjured him, as he regarded his fifter's life; that, not to make it appear fufpicious by too pofitive refufing, he wrote me a formal letter, and, at the fame time a private one, both (of which I am pretty fure are returned, and I can fhew you) and I anfwered him in the fame way: to Mr. Mylne I wrote a civil letter, telling him Mr. G. had informed me of his wifhes; that I was forry it was not in my power to fee his money paid which was due to him, as I had refufed taking adminiftration; but that if it was abfolutely neceffary, my regard for Mis. Mylne, who is indeed an amiable woman, would induce me to join with him in being fecurity to his creditors: however, he never, after writing me a letter of thanks, claimed any offer, and got abroad very well without it.

I con-

I confefs, I fhould not have thought it neceffary, or any part of my agreement, to tell you the reafon why I faw Mr. G. only every other night, had you not defired I would: it was fo agreed on between us, that by the intervention of one night, we might meet the next with more plea-fure, and have the lefs chance of being tired of each other. Not to mention, that as it was often four or five in the morn-ing before he went away, a night of fleep was abfolutely neceffary: as our converfa-tion was to be lafting, and I generally went to my room at eleven o'clock the night he came, which I thought would look odd, and fometimes put me to difficul-ties if I was at the Opera in a great croud, had company fupped with me, or any other hindrance; and I always contrived that fhould not be the cafe the nights he

came:

came : I faw him fome part of every day, or when I did not by any accident, he never failed writing.

A black inky kind of medicine (which I have mentioned before) occafioned two of my mifcarriages : the third, after trying the black medicine without effect, was occafioned by a vomit of emetic ; eating much pepper, and drinking a wine-glafs of brandy. I am afhamed to fay, I tried all thefe things the fourth time, without the fmalleft effect.

I do affure you, that no man ever took the fmalleft liberty with me (Lord S. yourfelf, and Mr. G. excepted) except three or four times that Mr. Stephens kiffed me, under one pretence or other; and once or twice that Mr. G. S. as we were ftanding

by

by the fire-fide, put his arm round my waift. Once, alfo, as I was admiring fome very fcarce and valuable plants at Hammerfmith, Mr. Lee told me, if I would allow him the honour to falute a Countefs, he would give me the moft curious; which I did, and had the plant. I recollect once, that Mrs. Stephens fitting on one of her hufband's knees, I fat on the other.

Mr. G. S. I know, was free in his way of thinking and acting; but his brother, I thought a different man, from fome things I had heard him fay; and which Mrs. Matra told me. Two or three times Mr. Stephens has come into my room, when my maid was dreffing my hair, and I took him into my bed-room, out of the drawing-room, where Mr. G. M. was to

fpeak about going off with Mrs. Stephens.

Many of the things thefe papers con-
tain, I have had an opportunity of telling
you fince I began to write them, which I
did not intend to do, till you read them
here : other things you have, in the courfe
of the fame time, told me you was thoroughly acquainted with; however I
would not alter, and I give you my
thoughts exactly, as they firft prefented
themfelves to me, as you will eafily perceive I wrote no rough copy.

My almoft ftarving myfelf to death at
Glamis ; my taking, in anger, almoft a
whole bottle of that black medicine ; my
foolifh behaviour about the cloaths and
favours I befpoke for Mr. Stephens's wed-
ding ;

ding; the dancings on that occafion; my allowing Mr. Stephens to call me his own wife; my worfe than foolifhnefs in going to St. Paul's with Mrs. Stephens and Mr. Pennick; and my making an excufe (with the laft defert of chriftening fome kittens) to have company to dine with me that day: all this knowing you are thoroughly informed of; I do not give more minutely than thus, on that account, nor fhould I have named them at all, had it not been for the oath's fake, which I could not fatisfy my confcience in taking, if I omitted, at leaft, mentioning, any one of even the moft trifling imprudencies I committed.

I have told you of Mr. C. W. having my hair and I his; and you know what a filly, though fhort refufal, I wrote to Mr. Mac Callafter, the autumn (I think it was)

was) before my marriage——To his laſt, I gave him no anſwer.

I have now fully performed my promiſe, and I rely on your's to excuſe all my faults, except want of veracity, which I am certain you cannot find here, and never ſhall again, even in the moſt trifling matter: as I will always rather prefer incurring your more than uſual ſhare of diſlike to me, than ſay what is not true.

You ſaw a bit of theſe papers laſt night, when you came into my dreſſing-room, though I begged you would not look, and was angry at my minuteneſs, and telling you ſuch trifles: if I had done otherwiſe, (beſides my oath) might you not with juſtice, and would you not have ſaid, I ordered you to be exact, minute, and ſcru-

N   pulous;

pulous; fo as to declare every thought that you had; were not thefe your own words? And how did you know what I fhould efteem trifling? Therefore, my deareft, you fhould excufe this minutenefs, and whatever manner I may mention the facts in, fo they be but facts!

God blefs you, and forgive me all my fins and faults.

FEBRUARY 3d, 1778. Tuefday morning.

I have had, you know, the paper you gave me in my pocket-book thefe three or four days; but, according to your orders, never looked at it till now. In confequence of what you there fay, I find myfelf obliged to fay fomething more about my fits, to which I did not intend, otherwife,

wife, to have added any thing. If I were to say, as you seem to require of me, that I ever could prevent or shorten them, and did not, except the one time I have mentioned, I should take my oath of a lie.

When I was a girl, I had two or three times obstructions, and then I took, as it were, common hysteric fits; but I never had them so violent, or any thing like convulsions, till four months that I had an obstruction after my second or third child, I forget which. And though my mind was perfectly easy at that time, I being in Scotland, and had always company that I liked, yet I suffered incredibly from these fits, both in health and looks; being exceedingly reduced and weakened. I really believe it was owing to Dr. Fergufon's prescriptions, and to the

easy

eafy ftate of my mind and good fpirits, that I recovered; but I have been fubject to them ever fince. Dr. Hunter knows, about three years ago or four, how much I fuffered in my looks from them; when he was fent for to me the day after I had been in one very bad, (no affectation) had you feen me after, you would have been convinced, would have affected a perfon both at the fame time and afterwards, as it has often done me. Sometimes when I have had warning, which is not often, I have ftopped the fit, by plunging my hands into cold water, and fometimes by drinking hot water or camomile tea. The time you went to Newcaftle; after that, when on your return you found me fo ill, I felt myfelf going to be ill; and having warning enough to drink a bafon of warm water, and plunging my hands in cold

water,

water, I prevented the fit coming on; but I never durft mention it till now, left you fhould fay it was an affectation or air that I gave myfelf.

What you fay Dr. Scott told you about my fits being pretended, and not a natural complaint, was as falfe, as I dare fay his faying my mifcarrying was, when I had that flooding, the firft time of my being regular after my lying-in; for you always took (at leaft I never perceived you did in the leaft otherwife) a moft certain precaution   I remember Dr. Scott afked me once, if not twice, whether I did not think I might have mifcarried; I faid, I could not tell, but thought only a flooding; for you may be fure, I would not hint, or even have him fufpect, that there was any reafon why I could not have mif-

carried.

carried. To the beſt of my recollection, he queſtioned me on this ſubject, one day when you brought him into the bed-room, and ſlipped yourſelf into the dreſſing-room for a minute, and not the moment I conclude you mean; that is, when he ſaying you ſent him, which you was angry at that time; upon the matureſt re-collection, I can venture to ſay, he did not aſk me that queſtion, or any other about my health, except in general terms, how I did; ſomething about my dinner, and mentioned the weather, or ſome ſuch ſubject: you wanted an explanation, or ſhould not have written this.

N. B. Though I do not recollect, I de-clare upon oath, Mr. Stephens kiſſing me oftener than I have mentioned; my ſit-ting on his knee oftener; or Mr. G. S.

putting

putting his arms oftener round my waiſt, and that was by accident; yet I have ſuch a dread of the poſſibility of perjuring myſelf, that I will not take my oath without a proviſo, I really believe a needleſs one, that they may have repeated theſe liberties oftener, but never any others; except Mr. Stephens ſhaking me by the hand.

May I never feel happineſs in this world, or the world to come; and may my children meet every hour of their lives unparalleled miſery, if I have, either directly or indirectly, told one or more falſehoods in theſe narratives; or if I have kept any thing a ſecret, that even Mr. Bowes could eſteem a fault.

This

This I give under my hand, and fhall never plead forgetfulnefs, or any thing elfe, for the truth of one tittle of it. And I do further fwear the truth of it upon the Holy Bible: and as a declaration of my fincerity, fhall take the Holy Sacrament upon it the next time I go to church, when there is one.

GIBSIDE, Feb. 3, 1778.

Examined with the Exhibit, contained in the Procefs tranfmitted from the Arches Court of Canterbury, this Fourth Day of October, 1788. By me, T. DODD, Clerk to Mr. Morley, Proctor, Doctor's Commons.

F I N I S.

CPSIA information can be obtained at www.ICGtesting.com
Printed in the USA
LVOW131926040212

267103LV00004B/68/P